Lao Tse

TAO TE CHING

Edition by Vladimir Antonov,
Ph.D. (in biology)

Translated into English by
Mikhail Nikolenko,
Ph.D. (in physics)

Corrector of the English translation —
Keenan Murphy

2nd Edition

2020

ISBN 978-1-927978-62-7
Published in 2020 by
New Atlanteans
657 Chemaushgon Road RR#2
Bancroft, Ontario
K0L 1C0, Canada

The book *Tao Te Ching* was written by the great Chinese spiritual adept, Lao Tse, about 2500 years ago. In that incarnation, Lao Tse was a disciple of non-incarnate Huang Di[1] and achieved full spiritual self-realization. At the present time, Lao Tse provides spiritual help to incarnate people.

The Tao Te Ching is one of the most fundamental texts on the philosophy and methodology of spiritual development.

http://www.swami-center.org
http://path-to-tao.info

_____

© Vladimir Antonov, 2020.

_____

[1] One can find more details in the book Classics of Spiritual Philosophy under the editorship of Dr. Vladimir Antonov.

1. One cannot cognize Tao[1] only by speaking about It.

One cannot use a human name to name that Origin of the sky and the earth — that Origin, Which is the Mother of everything.

Only those who are free from worldly passions can see It. And those who have such passions can see only Its Creation.

Nevertheless, Tao and Its Creation are One in essence, though They are called by different names. The passage which exists between Them is a doorway to all that which is miraculous.

2. When people know beauty, they then understand what is ugly.

When people learn what is good, they then realize what is evil.

In a similar way, existence and non-existence, hard and easy, long and short, high and low are pairs in which, by knowing one — a person then knows the other.

---

[1] Synonyms of this word of Chinese origin are Primordial Consciousness, Creator, God the Father, Ishvara, Allah, Svarog, etc.

In a similar way, there is a harmony that can be found between all preceding and succeeding pairs.

The wise prefer non-doing[2] and live in quietness[3]. Everything happens around them as if by itself. They are not attached to anything on the Earth.

The wise do not think that anything they have created belongs only to them. They do not feel attached to their own creations.

And since they do not exalt themselves, do not boast, and do not demand special respect from others, people find them pleasant to be around.

3. If the chosen are not exalted, no one envies them. If material treasures are not praised, no one steals them. In other words, if the objects of passions are not shown off, there are no temptations.

The wise ruler does not create such temptations for people, but ensures that people have enough food. This eliminates passions and strengthens people's health. Yes, by preventing temptations and passions in this way, even a deeply depraved person does not feel the need to commit evil acts.

---

[2] That is, the calm of mind and body, which includes the stopping of the flow of thoughts. It allows one to master the art of meditation and to develop oneself as a consciousness. (Those who are not accustomed to the word *non-doing* can mentally replace it with the word *meditation* when reading this text).

[3] Here Lao Tse means *inner quietness*, which is called *hesychia* in Greek. Hesychasm, an ancient tradition of the Christian mysticism, is named after it (see [6]).

The absence of all such passions and temptations brings calm.

4. Tao looks like a void and might be mistaken as being nothing. Yet, appearing to be nothing, It is omnipotent!

It is in the Depths.[4]

It is the Origin of everything.

It controls everything.

It pervades everything.

It manifests Itself as shining Light.

It is the Subtlest!

It is the Main Essence of everything!

One cannot describe Its origin, for It is Primordial.

5. Matter — both in the sky and on the earth — is dispassionate towards all creatures, be they plants, animals, or people; however, it is the base of all of them.

In the same way, the wise are dispassionate towards others.

The space above the earth is void and free, much like the space inside a bellows or a flute. And the more space there is for action, the more efficient the action can be.

---

[4] In the depths of multidimensional space. In other words, at the *subtle* end of the multidimensional scale.

The one who interferes with the actions of others and talks too much becomes unbearable for other people.

Therefore, it is always better to follow the principle of non-interference and keep inner calm.

6. The life and development of the Subtlest[5] are eternal and infinite.

It is the Deepest Base of everything.

On It the material world exists.

It acts without violence.

7. The sky and the earth are lasting. They last long because they exist not by themselves and not for the sake of themselves; they are created by Tao and exist for It.

The wise put themselves behind others; thus, they do not hinder other people and can lead them. The wise do not treasure the lives of their bodies; nevertheless, their lives are guarded by Tao.

This happens because the wise, too, exist here not for the sake of themselves. This is why their personal needs get realized for them.

The wise exist for Tao and serve It.

8. The wise live like water. Water serves all beings and does not require anything for itself. It exists below all things. In this respect, it is similar to Tao.

---

[5] Tao.

Life has to follow the principle of naturalness.

Follow the Path of the heart! Be friendly!

Tell only the truth!

When guiding others, follow the principle of being calm!

Every action has to be realizable and timely.

The one who does not strive to be ahead of others can avoid many mistakes.

9. One should not pour water into a full vessel. And there is no sense in sharpening the edge of a knife too much. And if a room is overfilled with gold and jade, who will guard it?

Excessiveness in anything causes troubles.

When the work is finished, one should retire.

Such are the laws of harmony suggested by Tao.

10. In order to maintain calm, one has to feel Unity with Everything[6]. Then, in particular, false egocentric desires cannot arise.

One has to refine the consciousness. Let one, in this respect, become similar to a newborn baby. The one who becomes this subtle becomes free from delusions.[7]

One has to rule the country and the people with love for them and without violence.

---

[6] To feel oneself as an integral part of the Absolute.
[7] Only through this can one cognize Tao.

The gate from the world of matter to the hidden world is open when one stays in calm. The understanding of this truth comes in non-doing.

To educate without violence, to make something without boasting, to create without feeling conceited about what was created, to be senior to others and not command them — this is the true righteousness of Great Te[8]!

11. Thirty spokes are united in one wheel. But the use of the wheel also depends on the space between the spokes.

Vessels are made of clay. Yet, their usefulness depends on the empty space inside them.

Buildings consist of walls, doors, and windows. Yet, the building's usefulness also depends on the space in it.

This is the relation between the usefulness of objects and emptiness.

12. The one who sees only five colors in the world is like the blind.

The one who hears only the sounds of the material world is similar to the deaf.

The one who partakes of only material food and feels only its taste is deluded.

---

[8] I.e., the higher ethics suggested by Te, by the Holy Spirit (Brahman).

The one who, in pursuit of prey, races at full speed is insane.

By accumulating jewelry and adornments, people act to the detriment of themselves.

The efforts of the wise are directed at having enough food, not at accumulating many objects. They, being satisfied with having little in the world of matter, choose *the Primordial*.

13. Glory and disgrace are equally feared. Fame is a great distress in life.

What does it mean that glory and disgrace are equally feared? It means that people fight for glory and then fear to lose it.

And what does it mean that fame is a great distress in life? It means that one suffers great distress because one treasures one's name.

When one ceases to treasure one's name, one will have no distress.

Thus, the wise do not seek praise from people. They just serve people self-sacrificingly; therefore, they can live among people in peace. They do not fight against anyone for anything; therefore, they are invincible.

14. If you try to look at Tao, you cannot notice It immediately. This is why It is called hard-to-be-seen.

If you try to listen to Tao, you cannot hear It immediately. This is why It is called hard-to-be-heard.

If you try to grasp Tao, you cannot hold on to It. This is why It is called hard-to-be-caught.

In Tao, are Those Who fill you with delight![9] And all Those in Tao are merged into One.

Tao is equal above and below.

However, Tao, infinite in size, cannot be called by the name of any One of Them.

They come out from Tao manifesting Their Individualities, then come back to the state without individual manifestations when They are again in It.

Tao has no corporeal image or face. This is why one regards It as hidden and mysterious.

Meeting Tao, I do not see Its face. Following Tao, I do not see Its back.

By strictly following the primordial Path of transformation of oneself as a consciousness, one can cognize the Eternal Origin. This Path is the Path to Tao.

15. Since ancient times, those who were capable of achieving spiritual Enlightenment successfully cognized the hidden and hardly recognizable small and large steps of this Path.

Such seekers were hard to recognize. I will outline their appearance: they were cautious like a man crossing a river in winter, they were circumspect because they were wary of strangers, they were alert be-

---

[9] Holy Spirits Who come out from Tao and Who are consubstantial to It. In the Christian tradition, They are called, in the aggregate sense, the Holy Spirit.

cause they knew that one's time on the Earth is limited, they were watchful as if they walked on melting ice, they were simple, they were vast like a valley, they were hidden from idle looks.

They were those who, in calm, could transform dirty into pure.

They were those who contributed to the Evolution of Life.

They worshipped Tao and they needed little in this world to be satisfied. Not desiring much, they were content with what they had and did not seek more.

16. Make emptiness[10] in yourself complete and achieve full calm! Let everything around you move by itself! Let everyone bloom spiritually and advance to cognition of their true Essence[11]!

Those who have cognized their true Essence achieve full calm. Thus, they attain the common Abode of All Those Who Have Attained[12].

One's presence in this Abode has to become constant. The One Who has achieved this goal is called Enlightened, Perfect, and the Possessor of the Higher Wisdom.

Those Who have attained that Abode represent the United We, which is the Highest Ruler. That Abode

---

[10] Here, it means the meditative state Nirodhi. In this state, the individual "I" completely disappears by dissolving in Tao.

[11] Atman, Higher Self, Tao.

[12] The Abode of the Creator.

is also called Heaven[13]. This is the Abode of Eternal Tao.

Tao is intangible. It cannot be "caught" by anyone. And therefore, It is invincible.

17. The Highest Ruler provides all Its people with the opportunity to develop themselves, as consciousnesses. But It does not seek to reward them with something worldly. It also does not try to inspire fear and awe in them.

Those who believe foolishly do not know about this. But those who have cognized It do not believe foolishly anymore.

This truth is so profound!

Having achieved success, I go even further, and a greater understanding about Everything opens up to me.

18. If people in a country deny Great Tao, they begin to talk about 'humanism' and 'justice'… But in this situation, these talks are nothing more than hypocrisy!

In a similar way, when there is discord in the family, then there arise demands of "filial obedience" and "parental love"…

And when in a whole country there is such disarray, there appear slogans of "patriotism" and "love for the motherland"…

---

[13] Or Heavens.

19. When falsity and hypocrisy of this kind are removed, people are much happier. Falsity, thirst for profit, theft, and cruelty towards living beings disappear when people possess true knowledge. It is so, because the reason for all people's vices is a lack of knowledge. It is knowledge that makes people understand that it is in their personal interest to be simple and kind, to control one's own worldly desires, and to liberate oneself from pernicious passions.

20. Cease to adhere to the objects to which you are attached, and you will be free from grief and self-pity! Only by living so, can one find the true Base[14] in life! Isn't this goal worthy of renouncing common beliefs and habits?

How great is the difference between good and evil!

Do not do anything undesired unto others. With this single principle, one can reduce chaos and establish order in society.

But now… all people indulge in vanity and society is immersed in chaos…

I alone stay calm and do not elevate myself over people. I am similar to a child who was not born in this world of vanity…

All people are bound by worldly desires. I alone have abandoned everything that they value. I am indifferent to all of this.

---

[14] Tao.

All people live in their egocentrism. I alone chose to get rid of it.

I flow as a Stream of Consciousness in Space and do not know when I will stop…

I cognize Tao in my heart! Oh, how subtle It is!

I am different from others in that I value That Which created our lives.

21. Te comes out from Tao. And Tao abides in the Primordial Depths.

Te is That Which acts and drives. It is as mysterious and hidden as Tao. Yet, It also exists!

It can assume a form.

It possesses Power. Its Power is superior to everything existing in this world.

Te can be seen. From ancient times to the present day, the Voice of Te sounds and tells the Will of the Creator of the entire material world.

Where can I see the countenance of Te? Everywhere!

22. Being satisfied with little, you can gain much. Seeking much, you will go astray. The wise heed this precept. If only all people would do so too!

The wise trust not only their material eyes; therefore, they can see clearly.

The wise do not think that they alone are right; therefore, they know the truth.

They do not seek glory, yet people revere them.

They do not seek power, yet people follow them.

They do not fight against anyone; therefore, no one can vanquish them.

They do not feel pity for themselves; therefore, they can develop successfully.

Only those who do not seek to be ahead of others are capable of living in harmony with everyone.

The wise care about everyone, and therefore they become an example to all.

They do not praise themselves, yet they are respected.

They do not elevate themselves, yet they are esteemed by others.

In ancient times, people said that the imperfect moves towards becoming perfect. Are these empty words? No! Truly, by achieving Unity, you will achieve Perfection!

23. Speak less and be simple!

Strong winds do not blow all morning. And strong rain does not continue all day long. What does this depend on? The sky and the earth.

The sky and the earth, though huge, cannot give birth to anything eternal. And neither can man. Therefore, it is better to serve Eternal Tao.

Those who serve Tao with their deeds receive the right to attain Mergence with It.

Those who have refined themselves[15] to the state of Te become coessential to Te.

Those who have refined themselves to the state of Tao become coessential to Tao.

Those who are coessential to Te gain the bliss of Te.

Those who are coessential to Tao gain the bliss of Tao.

But the unworthy one is deprived of this possibility.

It is unwise to doubt this truth!

24. The one who stands on tiptoes cannot stand for long.

The one who walks with long strides cannot walk for long.

The one who is seen by everyone cannot keep power for long.

The one who praises oneself cannot win glory.

The one who lives pitying oneself becomes weak and cannot develop.

The one who is envious cannot achieve success.

The one who exalts oneself cannot gain prestige.

The one who indulges in gluttony, does meaningless acts, and becomes irritated by everything cannot find peace.

---

[15] As a consciousness (soul).

Looking from Tao, one can see that all this is caused by vicious desires. All this is absurd behavior. Everyone turns away from such people.

On the contrary, the one who aspires to Mergence with Tao does not do anything like this.

25. Oh, That Which was born before the sky and the earth, living in calm, having no form, the Subtlest, the Only Existing One, Abiding everywhere, Boundless, Invincible, the Mother of everything, — You are called Tao. I also call You the Greatest! For You are eternal in Your infinite development!

Man, earth, and the sky depend on Tao. But Tao exists by Itself.

26. Hard work allows one to achieve an easy life in the future.

Yet, we also know that calm is the main thing in movement.

Therefore, the wise work hard all day long and do not avoid hard work. Nevertheless, while performing actions, they stay in the state of perfect calm.

They can even live in luxury and not get depraved by it.

So, why then is the owner of ten thousand chariots haughty and disdainful towards the entire world? Disdain destroys the soul!

And the absence of calm leads to a loss of the *Base!*...

27. The one who knows the Path can find the right direction even if there is no well-trodden trail. The one who knows how to speak does not misspeak. The one who knows how to count does not miscount. The best treasury has no lock, yet no one can open it. The best fetters are those which bind by nothing material, yet cannot be broken.

The wise know how to save people and save them constantly. The wise know how to help and do not leave anyone in trouble without help. Thus acts the deep wisdom!

The wise also instruct evil people so that such people can find the *Base*.

But if evil people do not value this help and do not want the *Base*, the wise leave them: the wise do not value relations with such people.

This principle is very important and profound!

28. If you are brave, be humble! And then the entire nation will follow you.

If you become a leader among people, let Great Te be your Guide. And be a pure, gentle, and subtle soul, like a child!

Abiding in good, do not forget about the existence of evil! And be an example of righteousness for everyone!

The one who becomes such an example for everyone in everything that has been said, no longer

differs by the quality of the soul from Great Te and then moves to Mergence with Eternal Tao.

Such a person, though knowing about his or her personal achievements and merits, chooses to be unknown, and thus becomes a wise leader.

It is favorable that such a wise person be a leader among people; then there will be order in such a country.

29. Some people have a great desire to rule the entire world, and they try to succeed in this aspiration. But I do not see how it can be possible, since the world is a container of wonderful and invincible Tao! And no one can rule Tao!

The one who aspires to this will surely fail!

Everyone has a choice: to oppose the harmonious flow of events or to follow it. The former struggle and lose strength, the latter bloom in the harmony and strengthen.

The wise never aspire to power, surfeit, luxuries, and prodigality.

30. A ruler faithful to Tao will not send an army to a foreign country. This would cause calamity to such a ruler in the first place.[16]

And the land through which an army passes becomes desolate. After a war, lean years come.

---

[16] At least, according to the *law of karma*.

A wise commander is never bellicose. A wise warrior never gets angry. The one who knows how to defeat an enemy does not attack. The one who has achieved victory stops and does not do violence to the defeated enemies. The victorious do not praise themselves. They win but do not feel proud. They do not like to wage wars. They win because they are forced to fight. They win even though they are not bellicose.

If a person, in the prime of life, begins to weaken and gets ill, this happens only because of living in disharmony with Tao. The life of such a person ends before the due time.

31. Weapons are a means that cause affliction; they must be discarded.

Therefore, the one who follows Tao does not use weapons.

Good leaders are yielding. They use power for defense only. They exert every effort to maintain peace.

To glorify oneself with a military victory means to rejoice over killing people. Is it right to respect those who are glad about killing?

Respecting virtue leads to wellbeing. But if one respects violence, then this leads to afflictions.

If many people are killed, it is a grievous event. The victory has to be "celebrated" with a funeral ceremony.

32. Tao is eternal and has no human appearance.

Though Tao is a tender Being, no one in the whole world can subjugate It.

If the nobility and rulers of a country lived in harmony with Tao, the common people would be peaceful and calm, the sky and the earth would unite in harmony, prosperity and wellbeing would come, and people would quiet down without orders!

For the sake of establishing order in a country, laws are created. Yet, the laws must not be too severe.

Leaders should be like Tao. Tao is like the ocean. The ocean is lower than all rivers, yet all rivers flow into it.

33. The one who knows people is reasonable. The one who has cognized oneself is enlightened.[17] The one who knows how to conquer enemies is strong. The one who has conquered oneself[18] is powerful.

The one who has material wealth is rich. The one who acts resolutely possesses willpower. But the one who indulges one's own desires is weak and foolish.

The one who attains Mergence with Tao and does not lose it also attains the Highest Existence. After

---

[17] I.e., the one who has cognized one's own multidimensional organism.

[18] I.e., the one who has conquered one's own vices, including their origin (the lower self with its egocentrism).

the death of the body, such a person continues to live in Tao as truly Immortal.

34. The Eternal Tao pervades everything. It is present to the left and to the right. Thanks to It, souls arise, live, and develop.

Though Tao is so Great and performs such great work, It does not seek to glorify Itself.

It raises all beings with love. It does not exert violence over them. It does not insist that people realize Its desires.

It is Great, though It does not insist on this.

Wise people aspire to It — to the Great!

35. All the Perfect Ones flow into Great Tao.

Follow this Path! By doing so you will not cause yourself any harm, on the contrary, you will achieve calm, harmony, and the fullness of life.

I, in the state of non-doing, travel in the Infinity of Tao. One cannot convey this with words! Tao is the Subtlest and most Blissful!

36. Worldly passions make man weak. Resoluteness fills man with power!

Worldly passions cripple man. Resoluteness elevates man and strengthens the consciousness!

Worldly passions enslave man. Resoluteness makes man free!

That which is dispassionate, gentle, and yielding conquers that which is passionate, hard, and coarse!

37. Tao does not act directly in the world of matter.[19] Yet, the entire Creation is a product of Its creativity.

Act in the same manner, and then all the living around you will develop in a natural way!

When you live with simplicity, not paying attention to gossip and hostile attitudes, and being in harmony with Tao, you then come to the state when you have no attachments and passions!

The absence of worldly desires brings one to the state of inner calm, and then order is established all around.

38. Those representing Great Te do not force Themselves to do good deeds: behaving righteously is natural for Them.

Those who are far from Te force themselves to perform good deeds: righteousness is not natural for them.

Those representing Great Te do not aspire to activity in the world of matter: They act in a state of non-doing.

Those who are far from Te live in vanity and act under the influence of their passions. In the religious aspect of life, their activity is reduced only to rituals.

---

[19] It is Te that acts.

But believing in the "magic" of rituals signifies the degradation of religion! Such people also force others to act like them.

This happens only to those who do not have Tao in their lives. They cannot be trusted. They have betrayed Tao and can betray anyone.

The wise who have cognized Tao are capable of distinguishing people by these features. They choose to communicate only with people of goodness.

39. There are Those Who have been living in Unity with Tao since ancient times. Thanks to Them, the sky is pure and the earth is stable, nature is gentle and rivers are full of water, valleys are covered with flowers, all living beings multiply, and the heroes of the spiritual Path are paragons of virtue. All this is provided by Those Who Have Achieved the Unity!

If They did not help, then the sky would cease to be pure and the earth would crack all over, nature would cease giving its beauty to all the living, valleys would stop blooming and turn into deserts, all living beings would stop multiplying and disappear, and the heroes of the spiritual Path would not be paragons of virtue and would be ridiculed and banished...

People are a base for their rulers. Therefore, those earthly rulers who elevate themselves do not have a strong base. This happens because they do not consider people as their base. It is their mistake.

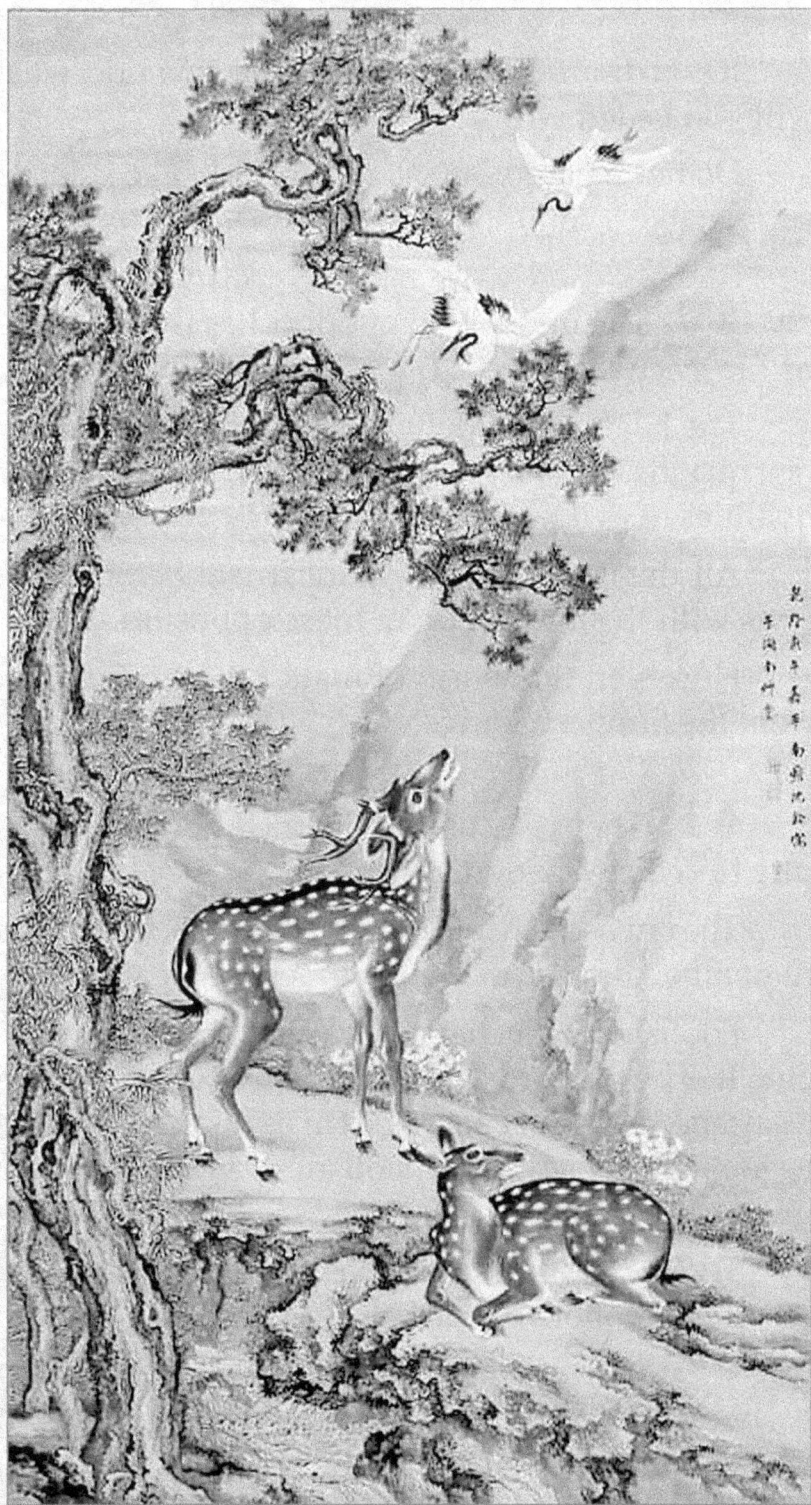

If you disassemble the chariot that you ride, what will you be left with?

Do not regard yourself as precious, like jade! Be simple, like a common stone!

40. The interaction of opposites is the sphere of Tao's activity.

The Highest Subtlety is one of the most important qualities of Tao. The opposite of This is the coarse qualities of evil people.

All the development of incarnate beings happens with the interaction of these opposites.

However, the world of matter itself originated from the Subtlest Source.

41. The wise, having learned about Tao, aspire to self-realization in It.

The unwise, having learned about Tao, sometimes remember about It and sometimes forget about It.

Foolish people, having learned about Tao, ridicule It. They regard Those Who have cognized Tao as insane… They regard wisdom as insanity…, higher justice as vice…, righteousness as depravity…, great truth as falsity…

Yes, the greatest square has no corners, the greatest sound cannot be heard, the greatest image cannot be seen…

Yes, Tao is similarly hidden from idle looks. It leads only those to Perfection who are worthy of it!

42. Once, One came out from Tao; after a time, He invited two Others; and those Two invited Three more. And all of Them then engaged in the creation on the planet of various forms of life.[20]

All creatures are subdivided into pairs of opposites — yin and yang — and are filled with chi. All further development comes from these interactions of opposites.

Everyone is afraid of loneliness and views it as suffering. This concerns earthly rulers as well.

They care only about themselves and refuse to help others.

However, the correct decision is to dedicate oneself to caring about others, thereby forgetting about oneself.

Wise spiritual seekers who dedicate their lives to the good of all will not be conquered by death. I prefer these words to all the other precepts of all the sages!

Those Who have attained Tao are merged into One in It.

43. It happens that the weakest defeat the strongest. The reason for this is that Te is present everywhere, pervades everything, and controls everything.

This is why I view non-doing as beneficial.

---

[20] Here, Lao Tse tells about several Holy Spirits (Te) Who guided the evolution of souls on our planet.

There is nothing in the world that can be compared, by its importance, to the teachings about inner quietness and the benefit of non-doing!

44. What is more necessary: life or glory? What is more valuable: life or wealth? What hurts more: gain or loss?

If you accumulate much, you will lose much!

Show moderation and you will avoid failures. Show moderation and there will be no risk. Thus, you can live life in calm, without worries!

The one who shows moderation does not suffer failure. The one who knows when to stop avoids affliction. Thanks to this, such a person can manage to cognize Primordial and Eternal Tao.

45. People may confuse the Greatest Perfection with insanity, great volume — with void, great curvature — with straightness, great humor — with foolishness, a great speaker — with the one unable to speak.

Intense movement overcomes cold. Stillness overcomes heat.

Only calm and harmony can ensure a correct understanding of everything that happens in the world.

46. If a country lives according to the laws of Tao, then horses are used for tilling land.

But if a nation renounces Tao, then war-horses run in the fields.

There is no greater affliction than uncontrolled worldly passions! And nothing destroys man more than the desire to multiply worldly treasures!

Those who know how to be content with what they have are always happy!

47. The wise cognize the world without leaving home. Without looking from a window, they see Primordial Tao. To learn more, they do not need to travel far.

The wise do not travel, yet know everything. They do not look, yet can describe everything. They seem to be non-acting, yet achieve everything.

In their hearts, they find everything that is necessary.[21]

This is why the wise know those things that are beyond material reach, without having to go and reach them physically. And they can see that which is invisible to the common eye.

48. They are those who learn to increase their knowledge every day. They are those who serve Tao decreasing their worldly desires. And by constantly

---

[21] Here, the author means not the material but spiritual heart, which is developed through the methods of Buddhi Yoga to a large size. Inside this heart, one cognizes Tao. From this heart, one finds ways leading to other beings.

decreasing worldly desires, one can achieve non-doing.

Only in non-doing can one master all the mysteries of the universe! Without non-doing, one cannot achieve this.

49. The wise have no selfish motives. They live in caring about others.

To good people I do good, and to the unkind I also wish good. This is the goodness of Te.

With honest people I am honest, and with the dishonest I am also honest. This is the honesty of Te.

The wise live in calm in their country. Yet, in the same land, other people live: both good and evil, honest and dishonest, reasonable and foolish, selfish and selfless, those who listen to Tao and those who deny It.

The wise, nevertheless, view all these people as their children.

50. People are born on the Earth and die. Out of ten, about a third continue onto paradisiacal existence, a third go to hell, and a third are those who have not succeeded in the development of the soul due to attachments to worldly affairs.

Those who have mastered the true life while living on the Earth are not afraid of rhinoceroses or tigers, and in battle, they are not afraid of armed soldiers. A rhinoceros has no place to plunge its horn into them, a tiger has no place to fasten its claws onto them, a soldier has no place to stab them with a sword. It is so, because to them there is no death![22]

51. Tao creates beings. Te nurses them, raises them, helps them to develop and mature, takes care of them, and supports them.

These beings gradually grow (as souls), develop, and achieve Perfection.

Therefore, there is no person who would not be obliged to worship Tao and Te.

Tao and Te coerce no one, They give all beings the possibility to develop naturally, according to their own freedom of will.

To create without feeling ownership of what was created, to make something without boasting, to be older than others and yet not command them — these are the principles of life of Great Te.

52. Everything in the material world has its Source, Which is the Mother of the material world.

When the Mother is cognized, it is easier to recognize Her Children[23].

---

[22] The one who has become a large spiritual heart (with the help of the methods of Buddhi Yoga) or who has even merged with Tao, quite naturally feels oneself as non-corporeal. Such a person — as a large consciousness — cannot be wounded by animals or weapons. Such a One is Immortal.

[23] Te.

Knowing the Children, one should not forget about the Mother. Then one lives life without troubles.

If one abandons personal desires and becomes free from worldly passions, then one lives without getting tired.

On the other hand, if one indulges in passions and becomes immersed in worldly affairs, then troubles are unavoidable.

To see the Subtlest is the true clearness of vision.

The preservation of the subtlety of the consciousness ensures true power.

Contemplate the Light of Tao! Cognize Its Depths! It is the true Treasure! Do not lose It, and you will avoid many troubles!

53. The one who possesses true knowledge walks the Straight Path.

The only thing that I am afraid of is to be absorbed in hustle and bustle.

The Straight Path is absolutely straight. Yet, people prefer… meandering trails.

If earthly rulers direct all their attention to the luxury of their palaces, then fields become overgrown with weeds, and granaries become empty. Such earthly rulers wear luxurious clothes and sharp swords, they are not satisfied with simple food, they accumulate too much wealth for themselves. This is equal to robbery and is a violation of the principles of life that are suggested by Tao.

54. By cognizing yourself, you cognize others. By helping others, you will cognize everything.

The one who can stand firmly cannot be overturned. The one who can lean against a support cannot be knocked down. Yes, such a person will be remembered by descendants!

When you achieve a similar stability in Tao, you will shine on others with Its Light, like the rising sun!

And help others to achieve the same stability; help your family, the people living in your country, and all people everywhere! By doing this, you will gain great power of the consciousness!

How have I cognized all this? In this exact way…

55. Those who live in Mergence with Great Te are pure, like newborn babies. Poisonous insects do not sting them, snakes do not bite them, wild animals and birds do not attack them. They have refined themselves as consciousnesses and are firmly merged with Tao.

They evaluate people not by their gender or by other outer qualities, but by looking at people's essence: at the soul.

They also perceive others as integral parts of the Whole[24], as parts of the Absolute.

And They possess the ability to initiate spiritual growth in people.

---

[24] More details can be found in [6].

41

They can preach all day long without straining their voice, because They stay in constant Mergence with Tao!

Such a life as this, is filled with happiness!

Common people, on the contrary, having reached the prime of life, immediately begin to fade into old age. It happens because they have not achieved Mergence with Tao.

56. The truth cannot be conveyed only through words! The one who does not understand this cannot fully understand this treatise![25]

Those who abandon personal desires, who become free from worldly passions, who reduce personal needs, who achieve clear understanding, who do not aspire to glory, who stay in the subtlest state of the consciousness, represent Primordial and Deepest Tao.

They cannot be tempted, offended, forced, or persuaded to seek glorification. No one can harm Them!

They shine like the sun! They are like a source from which everyone can drink!

They are the Highest Treasure among people!

57. From Tao, emanate calm, harmony, and justice.

Yet, among people, there is selfishness, guile, falsity, and violence…

---

[25] One can fully understand the truth only by realizing, in practice, everything that is described here.

宿雨清畿甸
朝陽麗帝城
豐年人樂業
壠上踏歌行

One can enter Tao only through non-doing.

When people strive to accumulate a multitude of unnecessary things, they become poor spiritually.

When they produce too many weapons, then robbery and disorder unavoidably arise.

When skilled craftsmen direct all their efforts at creating material valuables, then miraculous phenomena cease to happen in such a country.

When laws become too strict and repression becomes too great, then the opposition and the number of dissatisfied people grow.

This is why the wise abandon material fuss and let everything happen by itself.

One has to begin changing the world by changing oneself. If I aspire to quietness and calm, others become calm observing me. If I do not aspire to possessing many material boons, people around me also begin to be satisfied with having little. If I live without worldly attachments and passions, people around me also begin to living simply and naturally.

58. If earthly rulers rule in calm and harmony, the people, too, are calm and peaceful, and they do not feel the need to seek out better life conditions…

On the contrary, if earthly rulers act with irritation and aggressiveness, then the people begin to suffer. Then wellbeing is replaced with troubles and calamities. And people begin to seek a way out, and some of them find it by entering the state of non-doing and becoming immersed into the Light of Infinite Tao. Thus, luck and happiness may result from affliction.

As we can see, happiness and unhappiness give birth to each other…

The wise are always calm, gentle, and just. They do not want to take anything away from anyone. They are selfless and do not harm anyone. They are honest and live in harmony with Tao, nature, and other people.

They are bright but are not flashy.

59. In order to serve Tao successfully by helping other people, one needs to be able to preserve and accumulate one's power of the consciousness. This requires renouncing everything that wastes this power.

Such a renunciation at the higher stages of the Path helps one to grow one's own Power of Te, which can become inexhaustible and can help one to cognize Tao completely.

And Tao is the Eternal and Infinite Primordial Foundation of every person and of the entire material world. The pathway that unites man with this Foundation is called the root.

60. The activity of Tao and Te in relation to numerous individual souls of different ages can be likened to cooking a meal of many ingredients in a large cauldron.

In relation to the majority of people, when carrying out the destinies that these people deserve, Tao and Te use spirits, including spirits of lower levels of development.

But if one approaches Tao by the quality of the soul, then such a person goes beyond the sphere of influence of these spirits.

61. The Great Kingdom of Tao[26] is located as if behind the mouth of a river.

The Ocean is below all rivers, therefore all rivers flow into It.

The Ocean is calm and patient. It waits for Those Who will approach It and enter It.

The Ocean is the Great Kingdom. And on the Earth, there are small kingdoms composed of people.

The Great Kingdom takes care of satisfying all Those Who enter It.

So, let the rulers of small kingdoms also ensure that all their people are satisfied.

Then, all people will receive everything that they want, both in the Great Kingdom and in the small kingdoms.

And let us remember that those who are great should always put themselves below others.

---

[26] Also known as the Abode of the Creator.

萬壑爭流

62. It is Treasure of those good people who aspire to It. But, there are also evil people, and Tao acknowledges their role too.

Yes, one has to preach to all people about purity and kind behavior. However, are not evil people necessary?

Do they not help one to cognize the ephemerality of worldly treasures and the illusoriness of the hope to eternally stay on the Earth in one's present body?

Through interactions with them, do people not then desire to follow the path of goodness, desiring to become as unreachable to evil as possible? Indeed, in order to become unreachable to evil, one must perform concrete actions on developing oneself as a consciousness...[27]

Many people would not strive to become better if evil people did not "help" them!

Earthly rulers, possessing absolute power, and those closest to them value jewelry and luxurious chariots. However, in reality, they are not better than those who live in solitude and calm and who walk the Deepest Path to Tao! Would it not be better for those earthly rulers to start leading a calm life dedicated to cognition of Tao?

People say that in ancient times no one aspired to worldly wealth, and criminals were not executed. This is so, because, in those ancient times, people worshipped Tao.

---

[27] Such examples are given in [5,18].

63. Rid yourself of the bustle of the mind and unnecessary actions, keep calm, and be satisfied with simple food!

In this way, one begins walking the Path towards cognition of Great Tao, Which is the One Whole consisting of many Great Souls.

There are also many small souls that get incarnated into bodies.

Having understood this, the wise know that one should respond to hatred with kindness.

Start difficult work with an easy beginning. After all, every great work consists of small components. In this way — gradually — one fulfills great tasks.

If someone promises to perform great work quickly, then one should not trust the words of such a person…

But the wise never start "great undertakings" in the world of matter! This is why they can perform great work in the spiritual world. It is not hard for them.

64. It is easy to help those who have mastered harmony.

It is easy to show the way to a seeker who has not found it yet. However, one has to remember that a weak person can easily fall off the Path, and the one who is a weak soul will run away from difficulties.

It is better to begin constructing where you do not need to destroy old walls. It is better to introduce spiritual knowledge where you are not attacked by angry and foolish people.

And then, a great tree grows from a small sapling, a nine-story tower begins to be constructed from just a handful of earth, a journey of a thousand li begins with a single step.

In the world of matter, entrepreneurs go bankrupt, and property owners lose their property. This is why the wise do not act like this; and thus, they do not suffer failures. They possess nothing, and thus have nothing to lose.

The wise do not live in worldly passions. They do not strive to gain something material that requires much effort. They live in natural simplicity and are satisfied with what is refused by other people.

They walk the Path to Tao.

65. Those who have cognized Tao do not seek to put themselves "on display" in front of the ignorant. They also refuse to "rule the crowd"; and therefore, they can continue their personal development and continue helping deserving people.

Confidential higher knowledge about the methods of developing the consciousness can be harmful to people who are not ready to receive it.

The wise who know about this and act according to this knowledge, become examples for others.

觸袖野花多自舞
避人幽鳥不成啼

Thus acts Great Te.

In order to understand this, one has to recognize that Great Te is the Opposite of evil people. Great Te is located at an unreachable distance in relation to such people.

This is what Great Te is! It possesses the Highest Power and takes care of all the multitude of beings! It unites and separates people. It controls everything! It is the Ruler deserving the strongest love and respect!

By learning from It, you will achieve the highest wellbeing!

66. Great rivers are so powerful because they flow down into the sea, accumulating in themselves water from all around.

Likewise, the wise who desire to help people have to put themselves below others. This is why, despite being superior, they are not a burden to people. And it also why people do not seek to harm them. People gladly follow them and do not turn away from them.

They do not compete with anyone; therefore, they are unconquerable.

They constantly advance further, yet people do not envy them.

They do not struggle against anyone, and thus no one in the whole world can force them to act against their will.

67. Tao is Great and has no equals or anything similar to It!

It resides so deeply and is so subtle that no one can "catch It" or force It to do something!

I possess three treasures that I value: the first is love for people, the second is frugality, and the third is that I do not desire to be ahead of others. I love people; thus, I can be brave. I am frugal; thus, I can be generous. I do not desire to be ahead of others; thus, I can be a wise leader.

All those who are brave but do not love, who are generous without being frugal, or who try to be ahead of others and push others away, suffer failure.

On the contrary, those who are full of love achieve victory and become unconquerable because Tao constantly guards such people.

68. A wise leader is never bellicose. A wise soldier never gets angry. The one who knows how to win does not attack first. The one who knows how to lead people does not humiliate them, but puts oneself in a lower position.

Such are the laws of Te about rejecting anger, self-praise, and violence. This is how act Those Who represent Te and guide people to Primordial and Eternal Tao.

69. Military art teaches: I do not begin first, I have to wait. I do not advance even an inch, but rather retreat a foot. This is called acting without action, winning without violence. In this case, there will be no enemies; and thus, I can avoid wasting power.

There is no affliction worse than hating enemies! Hatred towards enemies is the path leading to the loss of the most important One: Tao!

Therefore, those who avoid battles come out victorious.

70. My words are easy to understand and realize. Yet, many people cannot understand them and cannot realize them.

Behind my words, there is the Origin of everything. However, since those people do not know It, they also do not understand me.

The one who has cognized Tao is quiet and unnoticeable, yet behaves with dignity. Such a person wears simple clothes and hides the treasure[28] within.

71. The one who possesses knowledge, but knows how and when to keep silent about it, is honorable.

The one who has no knowledge, yet pretends to know, is not healthy.

Those who are wise heal themselves. The wise never fall ill because they rid themselves of the causes of illnesses. They abide in Tao. How can they be ill then?

---

[28] Wisdom.

72. The one who lives in fear cannot become strong. The strength of the consciousness can only be gained if one lives without fear.

Also, rid yourself of the ability to despise others! The one who despises others is despicable in front of Tao!

Rid yourself of violence in relations with others! The one who does violence to others will be subjected to violence.

Renounce the ability to deceive people! The one who deceives others, deceives oneself.[29]

Live in love!

Do not strive to show yourself off! The one who has cognized one's own Higher Essence is not engaged in self-admiration and does not elevate oneself above others.

The one who has rid oneself of egocentrism gains an opportunity to achieve Tao.

73. The one who is brave and bellicose will be killed. The one who is brave but is not bellicose will live.

What is the reason for disliking bellicose people? Even a sage has difficulty explaining it.

Great Tao abides in calm. It does not fight against anyone. It wins without violence.

---

[29] Because such a person does not take into account God and His principles of the formation of people's destinies.

Great Tao is silent, yet It answers questions and comes to those who call It.

In calm, Great Tao controls everything.

Great Tao selects worthy people into Itself.

74. It makes no sense to threaten to kill a person who is not afraid of death.

But the one who threatens others with death and takes pleasure in this will be destroyed.

Life and death are under the control of Tao alone. No one is allowed to control this instead of Tao! The one who decides to do such a thing only harms oneself.

75. Looking at the majority of people, one may think that they are constantly hungry. For they are always concerned with the accumulation and multiplication of their supplies and they cannot stop in this activity!

In all affairs, they aspire only to personal profit, by any means!

They do not understand the principles of life suggested by Tao about loving others and caring about them. And they also do not understand Its principle about non-doing.

They live without looking at Tao, ignoring Tao, wasting their vital force doing things that have no true value. Their "love for life" is too strong; therefore, they die too early.

On the contrary, those who pay little attention to their own earthly lives, being so completely engaged in the common good, increase the value of their lives before Tao.

76. The human body at birth is gentle and flexible, but after death it becomes hard. All vegetal beings are also gentle and flexible at birth, but after death they become dry and brittle.

A powerful tree either breaks in a storm or is cut down by an axe. A flexible and gentle tree has an advantage here.

The one who is gentle and flexible walks the path of life. The one who is not gentle and flexible walks the path of death.

77. Let the Life of Primordial Tao be an example for us!

The one who does violence to people, who humiliates and robs them, opposes Tao.

But the one who never acts selfishly, who gives one's own surplus to others, who performs deeds not for the sake of glory, who lives with calm and without worldly passions, who submerges into the tender and subtle calm of Tao and helps deserving people on this Path, — such a person becomes similar to Tao.

78. Water is gentle and yielding, yet it erodes away that which is hard. Nothing compares to it in overcoming that which is hard.

Gentle and tender overcome hard and coarse. Only wise people understand the essence of this statement…

79. A big emotional disturbance has consequences. That is why calm can be regarded as good.

And, therefore, the wise give an oath not to condemn anyone.

Kind people live in accordance with this rule; evil people do not.

Primordial Tao is always on the side of kind people.

80. About the state structure, I think the following:

It is good if a country is small and its population is sparse.

Even if there are many weapons, they should not be used. War ships and chariots should not be used either. Warriors should not wage war.

It is necessary that life in a country be such that people do not seek to leave the country.

It is good if everyone has tasty food, beautiful clothes, cozy houses, and a joyful life.

It is good to look with love at neighboring states, and to listen to how roosters crow there and dogs bark.

It is good if people, having reached an old age, cognize Perfection before leaving this world, thus no longer needing to return here again.

81. The right words are not necessarily elegant. Beautiful words are not necessarily trustable.

A kind person is not necessarily eloquent. An eloquent person is not necessarily kind.

The one who knows — does not argue. The one who argues — does not know.

The wise are not selfish, they act for the good of others.

Great Tao is concerned about the welfare of all living beings. Everything that Tao does towards living beings does not contain violence and does not harm anyone.

The wise also act without violence and do not harm anyone.

Recommended books:

1. Antonov V.V. — Agni Yoga. "New Atlanteans", Bancroft, 2008.

2. Antonov V.V. — Atlantis and the Atlanteans (The Emerald Tablets and Other Texts). "New Atlanteans", Bancroft, 2008.

3. Antonov V.V. — Bhagavad Gita with Commentaries. "New Atlanteans", Bancroft, 2008.

4. Antonov V.V. — The Beauty of Pure Islam. "New Atlanteans", Bancroft, 2008.

5. Antonov V.V. — Classics of Spiritual Philosophy and the Present. "New Atlanteans", Bancroft, 2008.

6. Antonov V.V. — Ecopsychology. "New Atlanteans", Bancroft, 2008.

7. Antonov V.V. — Forest Lectures on the Highest Yoga. "New Atlanteans", Bancroft, 2008.

8. Antonov V.V. — The Gospel of Philip. "New Atlanteans", Bancroft, 2008.

9. Antonov V.V. — The Original Teachings of Jesus Christ. "New Atlanteans", Bancroft, 2008.

10. Antonov V.V. — Patanjali's Ashtanga Yoga: from Theory — to Practical Realization. "New Atlanteans", Bancroft, 2008.

11. Antonov V.V. — Pythagoras and His School. "New Atlanteans", Bancroft, 2008.

12. Antonov V.V. — Sathya Sai Baba – the Christ of Our Days. "New Atlanteans", Bancroft, 2007.

13. Antonov V.V. — Sexology. "New Atlanteans", Bancroft, 2008.

14. Antonov V.V. — Spiritual Work with Children. "New Atlanteans", Bancroft, 2008.

15. Antonov V.V. — The Teachings of Babaji. "New Atlanteans", Bancroft, 2008.

16. Antonov V.V. — The Teachings of Don Juan Matus. "New Atlanteans", Bancroft, 2008.

17. Antonov V.V. — Sexology. "New Atlanteans", Bancroft, 2008.

18. Antonov V.V. — How God Can Be Cognized. Autobiography of a Scientist Who Studied God. "New Atlanteans", Bancroft, 2009.

19. Antonov V.V. — Anatomy of God. "New Atlanteans", Bancroft, 2010.

20. Antonov V.V. — Life for God. "New Atlanteans", Bancroft, 2010.

21. Antonov V.V. — Spiritual Heart. The Religion of Unity. "New Atlanteans", Bancroft, 2010.

22. Antonov V.V — Anatomy of God. "New Atlanteans", Bancroft, 2014.

23. Antonov V.V — "Bubbles of Perception". "New Atlanteans", 2015.

24. Antonov V.V — God-centrism. "New Atlanteans", 2015.

25. Antonov V.V — Teachings of God. "New Atlanteans", 2016.

26. Antonov V.V. — To Understand God. "New Atlanteans", Bancroft, 2020.

27. Antonov V.V., Zubkova A.B. — Taoism. "New Atlanteans", Bancroft, 2013.

28. Zubkova A.B. — Divine Parables. "New Atlanteans", Bancroft, 2008.

29. Zubkova A.B. — Divine Stories of Slavic Lands. "New Atlanteans", Bancroft, 2013.

30. Zubkova A.B. — Dialogues with Pythagoras. "New Atlanteans", Bancroft, 2008.

31. Zubkova A.B. — Dobrynya. Bylinas. "New Atlanteans", Bancroft, 2008.

32. Zubkova A.B. (comp.) — Book of the Born in the Light. Revelations of the Divine Atlanteans. "New Atlanteans", Bancroft, 2008.

33. Zubkova A.B. — Parables of Lao Tse. "New Atlanteans", Bancroft, 2011.

34. Zubkova A.B. — Parables about the Elder Zosima. "New Atlanteans", Bancroft, 2013.

35. Zubkova A.B. — Story about Knyaz Dmitry and Volhva. "New Atlanteans", Bancroft, 2013.

36. Zubkova A.B. — Story about Princess Nesmeyana and Ivan. "New Atlanteans", Bancroft, 2007.

37. Zubkova A.B. — Sufi Parables. "New Atlanteans", Bancroft, 2014.

38. Zubkova A.B. — Lessons of Pythagoras. "New Atlanteans", Bancroft, 2016.

39. Zubkova A.B. — Fairy Tales of Kindness, "New Atlanteans", Bancroft, 2016.

40. Zubkova A.B. — Kind Fairy Tales. "New Atlanteans", Bancroft, 2017.

41. Zubkova A.B. — The Saga of Odin. "New Atlanteans", Bancroft, 2020.

42. Zubkova A.B. — The Gospel of Martha. "New Atlanteans", Bancroft, 2020.

43. Spalding B. — Life and Teaching of the Masters of the Far East. "DeVorss & Co", 1924.

44. Tatyana M. — On the Other Side of the Material World. "New Atlanteans", Bancroft, 2012.

45. Katerina O. — The Master. "New Atlanteans", Bancroft, 2020.

46. Teplyy A.B. (comp.) — Book of the Warrior of Spirit. "New Atlanteans", Bancroft, 2008.

Our video films:

1. *Immersion into Harmony of Nature. The Way to Paradise.* (Slideshow), 90 minutes (on CD or DVD).

2. *Spiritual Heart.* 70 minutes (on DVD).

3. *Sattva (Harmony, Purity).* 60 minutes (on DVD).

4. *Sattva of Mists.* 75 minutes (on DVD).

5. *Sattva of Spring.* 90 minutes (on DVD).

6. *Art of Being Happy.* 42 minutes (on DVD).

7. *Keys to the Secrets of Life. Achievement of Immortality.* 38 minutes (on DVD).

8. *Bhakti Yoga.* 47 minutes (on DVD).

9. *Kriya Yoga.* 40 minutes (on DVD).

10. *Practical Ecopsychology.* 60 minutes (on DVD).

11. *Yoga of Krishna.* 80 minutes (on DVD).

12. *Yoga of Buddhism.* 130 minutes (on DVD).

13. *Taoist Yoga.* 91 minutes (on DVD).

14. *Ashtanga Yoga*. 60 minutes (on DVD).

You may order our books and films at the Lulu e-store:

https://www.lulu.com/shop

and at Amazon:

https://www.amazon.com/Vladimir-Antonov/e/B002BM5BF4

You can also download for free our films, screen-savers, printable calendars, etc from the site:

www.spiritual-art.info

Visit www.swami-center.org for our books, photo gallery, and other materials in different languages.

The paintings in this publication of Tao Te Ching are by Qian Du, Leng Mei, Tang Yin, Ma Yuan, Shen Quan, Wang Shimin, Ma Yuan, Lü Ji, Gao Cen, Hua Pinshan, Pan Gongshou, Wang Hui, and Wang Jian.

Amazon.com

Lulu.com

SwamiCenter

Design by
Ekaterina Smirnova.

www.ingramcontent.com/pod-product-compliance
Lightning Source LLC
LaVergne TN
LVHW091209080426
835509LV00006B/913